ELTON JOHN
FAVORITES

ISBN 978-1-4584-1728-2

HAL•LEONARD®
CORPORATION

7777 W. BLUEMOUND RD. P.O. BOX 13819 MILWAUKEE, WI 53213

Visit Hal Leonard Online at
www.halleonard.com

BLESSED

Words and Music by ELTON JOHN
and BERNIE TAUPIN

Moderately

To Coda ⊕

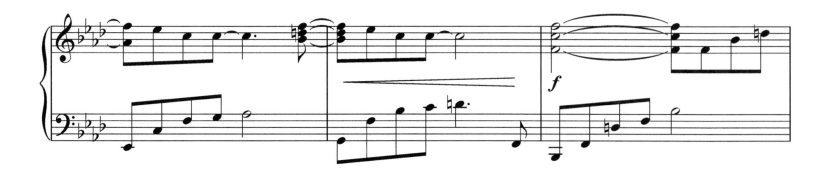

D.S. al Coda

CODA

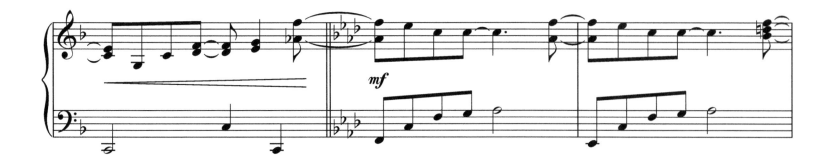

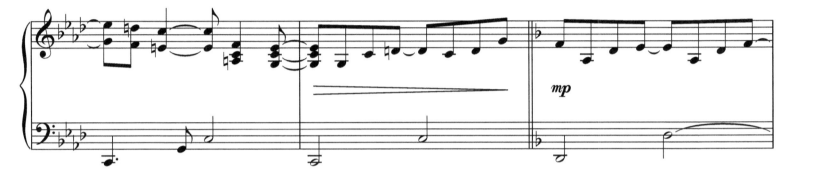

CANDLE IN THE WIND

Words and Music by ELTON JOHN
and BERNIE TAUPIN

Moderately slow, in 2

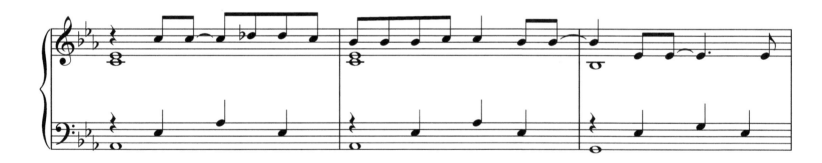

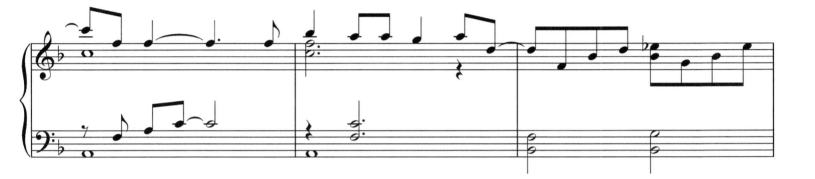

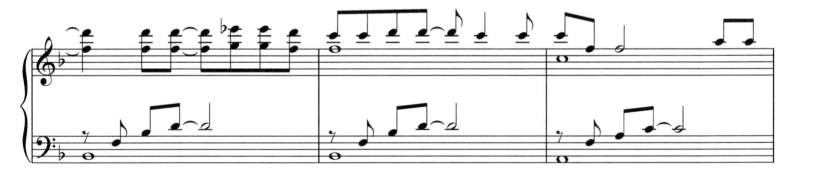

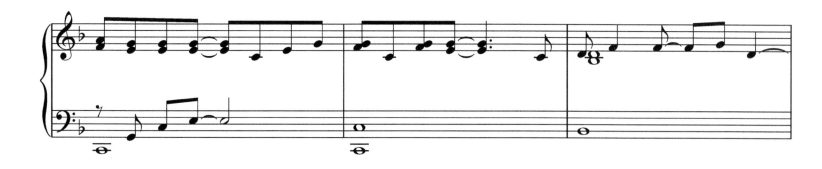

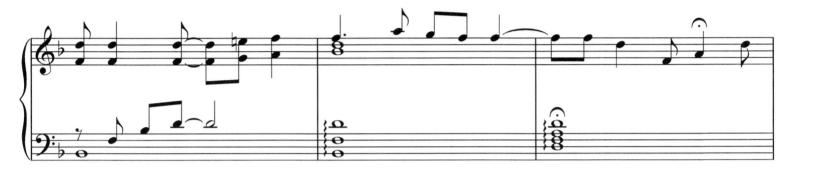

DON'T LET THE SUN GO DOWN ON ME

Words and Music by ELTON JOHN
and BERNIE TAUPIN

Moderately slow

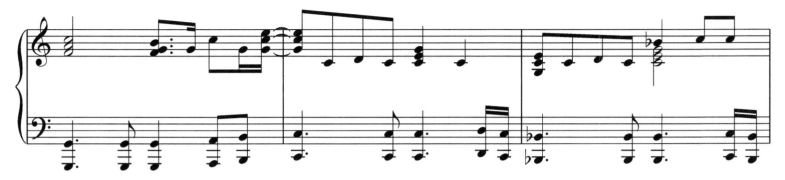

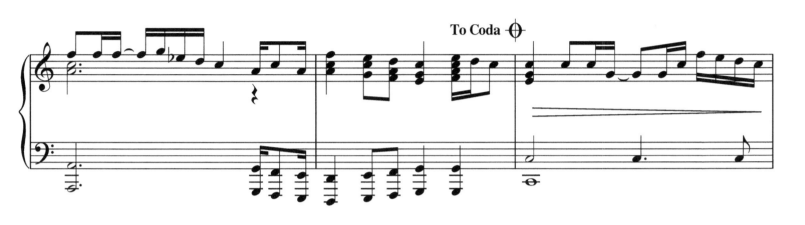

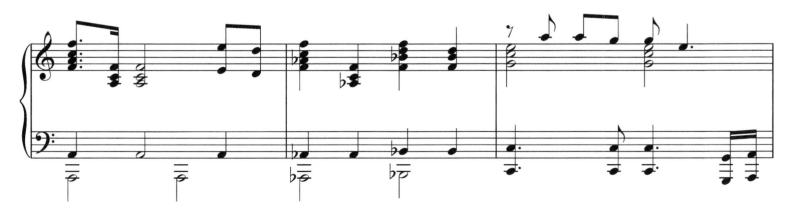

LUCY IN THE SKY WITH DIAMONDS

Words and Music by JOHN LENNON
and PAUL McCARTNEY

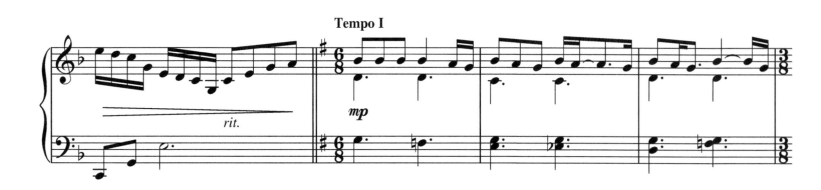

Steady four

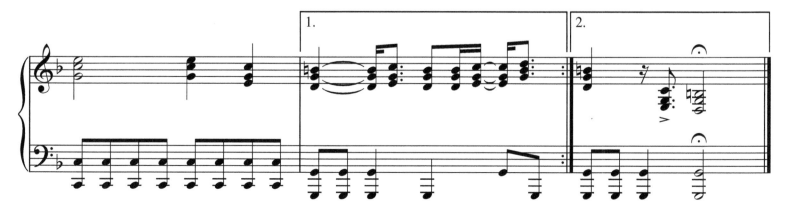

I WANT LOVE

Words and Music by ELTON JOHN
and BERNIE TAUPIN

To Coda ⊕

D.S. al Coda

CODA

NIKITA

Words and Music by ELTON JOHN
and BERNIE TAUPIN

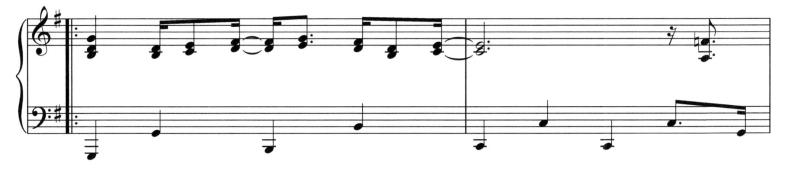

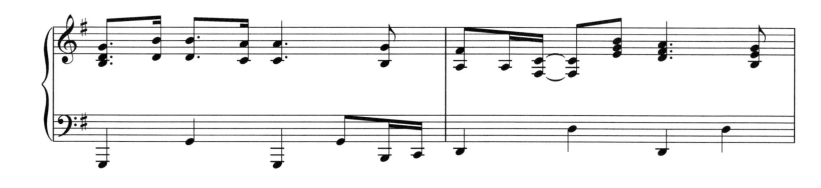

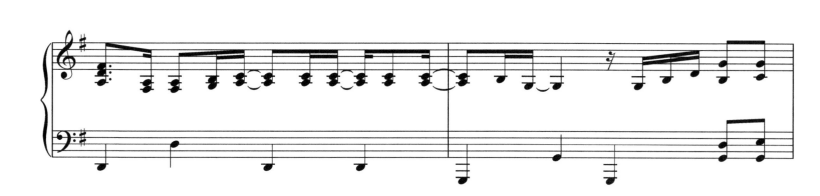

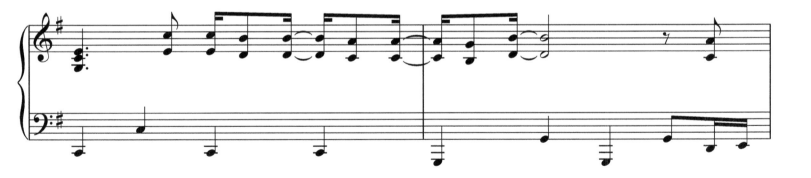

To Coda ⊕

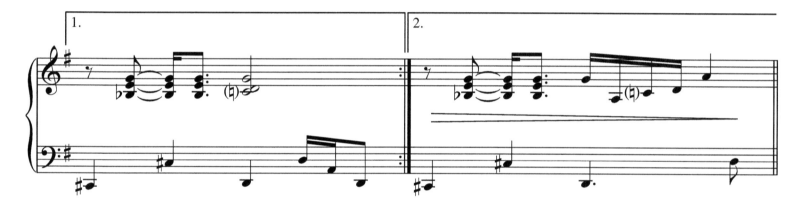

34

CODA

SOMETHING ABOUT THE WAY YOU LOOK TONIGHT

Words and Music by ELTON JOHN
and BERNIE TAUPIN

Moderately slow, in 2

With pedal

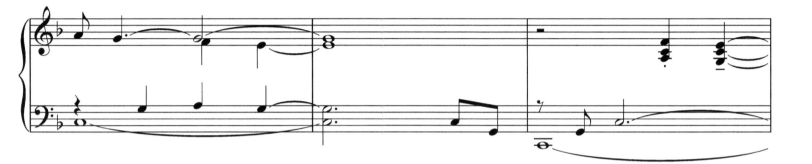

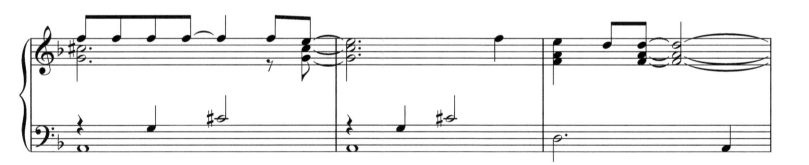

To Coda

dim. *mf*

D.S. al Coda

CODA

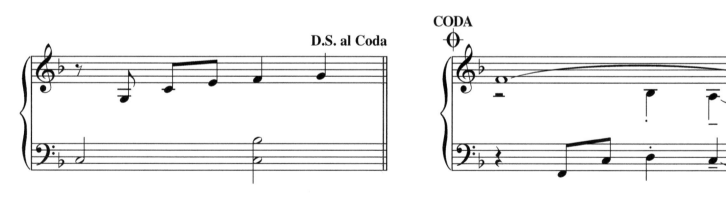

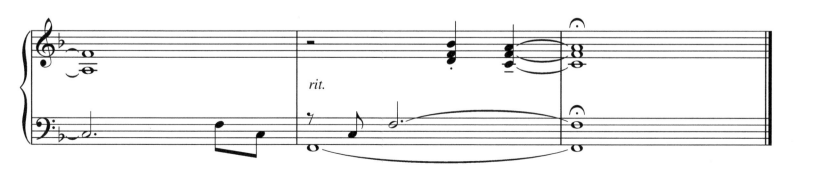

rit.

SOMEDAY OUT OF THE BLUE
(Theme from El Dorado)
from THE ROAD TO EL DORADO

Music by ELTON JOHN and PATRICK LEONARD
Lyrics by TIM RICE

Moderately, in 2

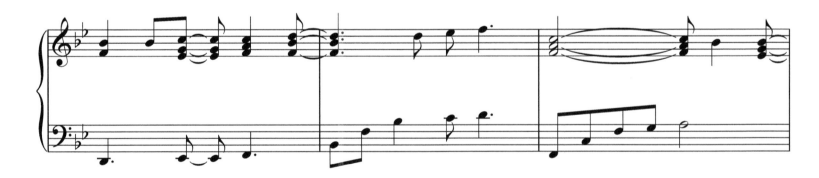

To Coda

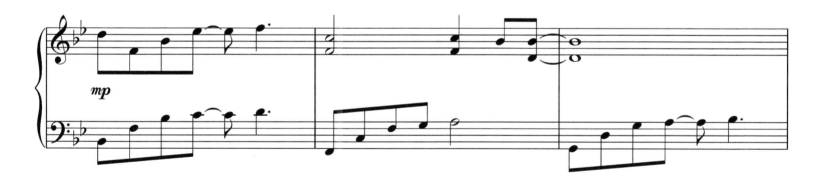

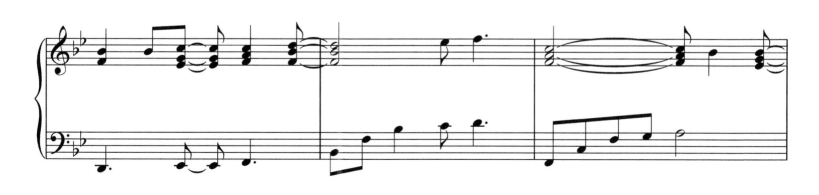

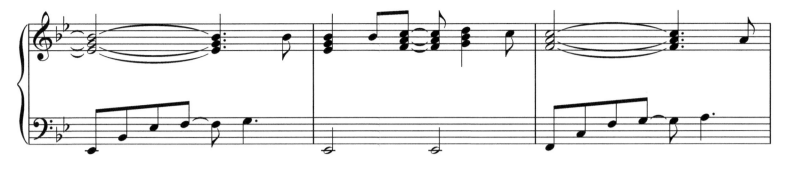

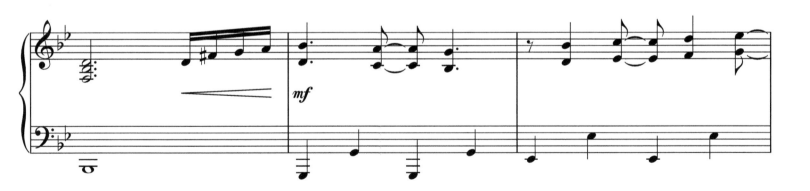

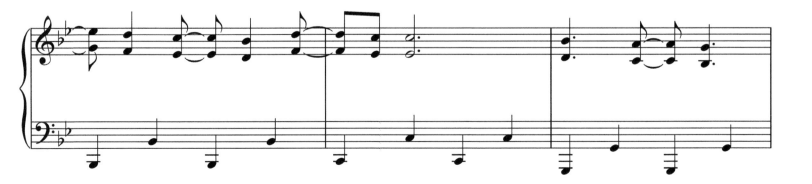

D.S. al Coda

CODA

SORRY SEEMS TO BE THE HARDEST WORD

Words and Music by ELTON JOHN
and BERNIE TAUPIN

Gently, in 2

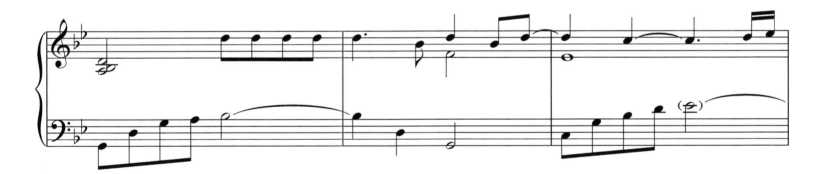

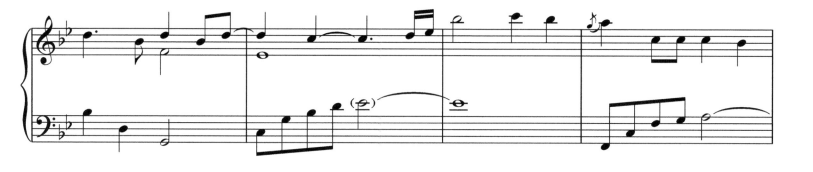

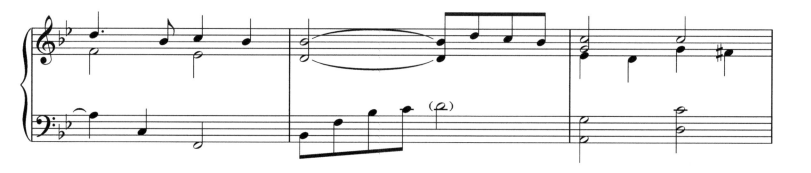

To Coda

D.S. al Coda

CODA

mp

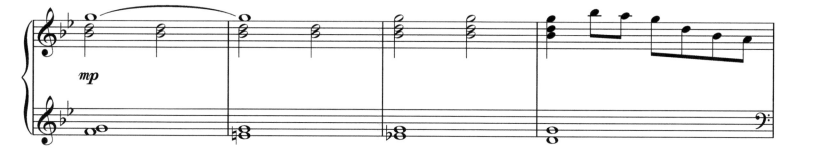

TINY DANCER

Words and Music by ELTON JOHN
and BERNIE TAUPIN

Moderately, in 2

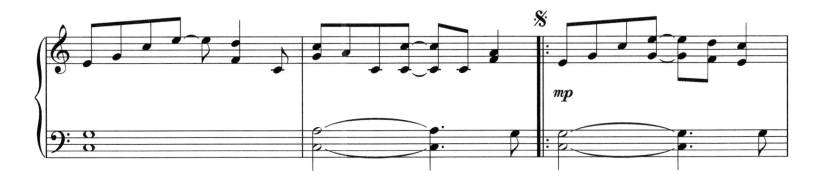

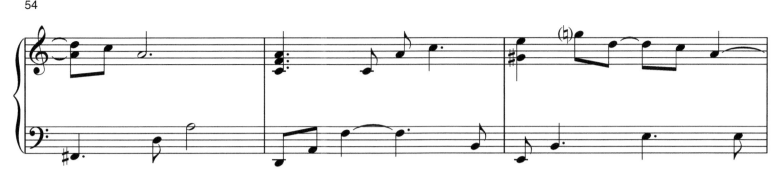

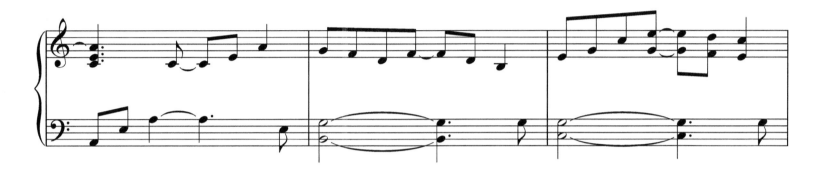

To Coda ⊕

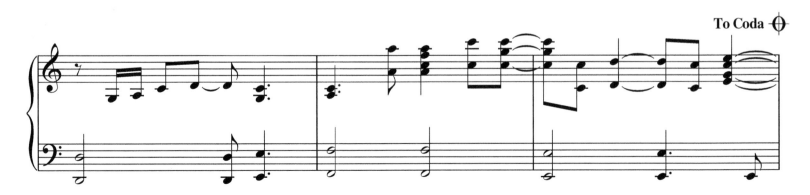

D.S. al Coda
(take 2nd ending)

CODA

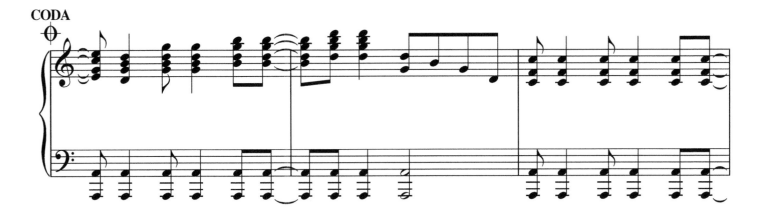

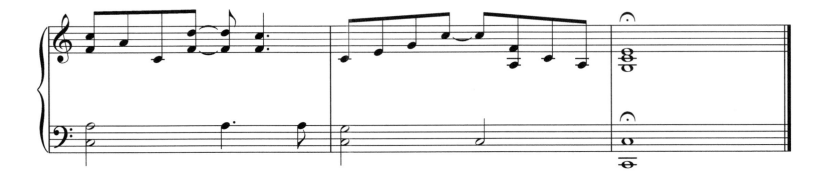

YOUR SONG

Words and Music by ELTON JOHN
and BERNIE TAUPIN

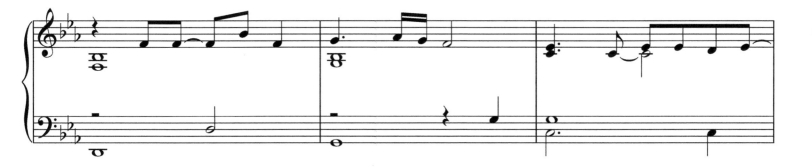

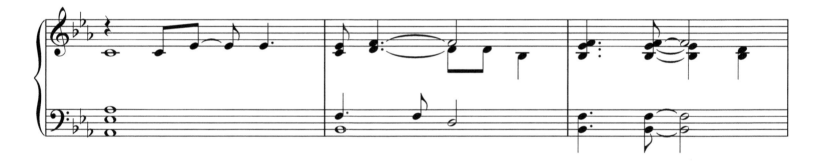

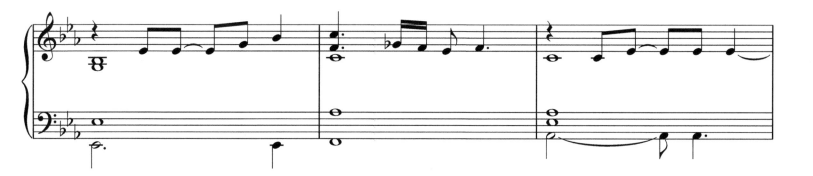

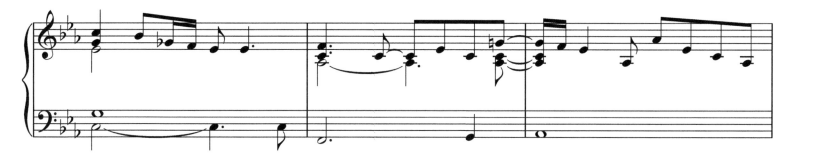

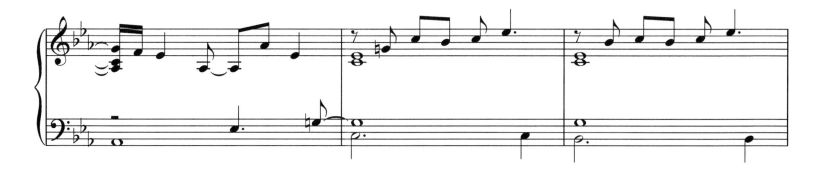

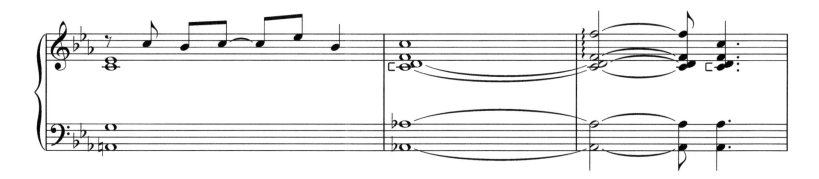

To Coda

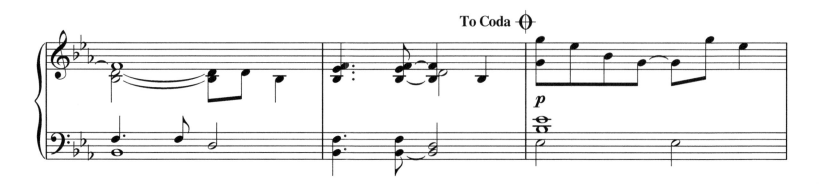

D.S. al Coda

CODA

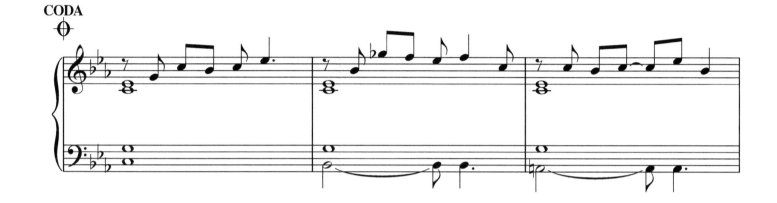

rit.